GOD'S STRATEGY IS SUPERIOR

When His Way Doesn't Make Sense—But Works
(Based on Judges 7, the Story of Gideon)

PASTOR DR. CLAUDINE BENJAMIN

For more information or to book an event, contact:
inspiredtowinsouls@gmail.com

Published by:

Editor: Cleveland O. McLeish (Author C. Orville McLeish)

ISBN: 978-1-965635-72-8 (paperback)

ABOUT THE AUTHOR

Pastor Claudine Benjamin is a devoted servant of God, a powerful voice in the body of Christ, and a passionate teacher of the Word whose life and ministry reflects deep surrender to God's will. Known for her prophetic insight, compassionate leadership, and bold declarations of truth, she has dedicated her life to equipping the church to walk in obedience, even when the path doesn't make sense.

With a heart for those who feel hidden, broken, or underqualified, Pastor Claudine speaks directly to the Gideons of this generation—those whom God is calling out of the winepress and into their divine assignment. Her message is one of radical faith, divine strategy, and full dependence on the sovereignty of God.

Her teachings, books, and ministry events are marked by a unique anointing to bring clarity in seasons of confusion and to draw believers into deeper trust when God's instructions seem unconventional.

As the author of numerous Spirit-led books focused on spiritual transformation, purpose, and revival, Pastor Claudine continues to sound the trumpet for the church to return to obedience, intimacy with God, and kingdom alignment.

She believes wholeheartedly that God's way is still the best way, even when it requires walking by faith, not by sight.

DEDICATION

This book is dedicated to every believer who has ever questioned the process, doubted the path, or felt overwhelmed by God's unusual instructions.

To the Gideons of this generation—those who feel underqualified, outnumbered, and hidden in the winepress—may you discover that you are exactly who God is calling to lead, to rise, and to conquer.

May you never be discouraged by what doesn't make sense, because God's strategy is not based on sense—it's built on sovereignty.

You are proof that less is never lacking when God is in it. Stay surrendered, stay obedient, and stay positioned.

ACKNOWLEDGMENT

To my sovereign God, this book is Yours from beginning to end. Thank You for being faithful when I wasn't certain, and for unfolding Your divine plan, even when I didn't fully understand it. May every word bring glory to You and build the faith of those who read it.

To every intercessor, mentor, spiritual leader, and friend who encouraged me to finish what I started, thank you for reminding me that obedience always bears fruit, even in the waiting.

To those who've walked with me through seasons of divine reduction, strategic pruning, and unconventional leading, thank you for believing when I had nothing but a trumpet, a jar, and a torch.

To the readers, thank you for allowing this message into your journey. My prayer is that these pages not only encourage your heart, but also align your life with heaven's direction. May you embrace God's strategy, even when it doesn't make sense, because it works.

TABLE OF CONTENTS

INTRODUCTION

WHEN LOGIC FAILS BUT GOD PREVAILS

There comes a moment in every believer's life when logic runs out—when your experience, intellect, and natural senses no longer provide answers, and the only option is to trust in something higher, deeper, and greater than yourself.

That's where God's strategy begins.

Because while human plans rely on strength, numbers, reason, and predictability, God often chooses what seems illogical to reveal His power, His purpose, and His glory.

This book is born out of that very paradox: when what God asks you to do seems to contradict everything you've been taught about success, strength, and strategy but still leads to undeniable victory.

WHY GIDEON? WHY NOW?

In Judges 6 and 7, we find a man named Gideon, who was neither a general nor a warrior, and who lacked confidence. He was hiding in fear when God called him a **"mighty man of valor."** He didn't believe in himself. He questioned God's call. He put out fleeces. He was unsure every step of the way.

And yet—he obeyed.

And through that obedience, God reduced his army from 32,000 to 300, gave him a battle plan that required no weapons, and delivered Israel with a strategy that no man could have imagined but that no enemy could withstand.

Gideon's story speaks loudly to our generation because we are facing spiritual, emotional, and personal battles where logic isn't enough. Traditional methods are failing. Comfortable solutions are no longer effective. We are being forced to choose between control and trust, between human reasoning and divine instruction.

WHAT YOU CAN EXPECT FROM THIS BOOK

This book is a journey through Judges 6–7, chapter by chapter, lesson by lesson, exploring how God:

- Calls the unqualified.
- Confronts idolatry before destiny.
- Reduces before He releases.
- Reveals victory through brokenness.
- Fights battles in unexpected ways.

Each chapter ends with Reflection Questions, a Faith Declaration, and a Prayer to help you apply these principles to your own walk with God.

Whether you are in a season of hiddenness, reduction, testing, or stepping into a battle that seems too big for you, you are not alone, and you are not unprepared. You are simply being positioned for a greater revelation of God's superior strategy.

WHEN LOGIC FAILS, YOU'RE IN THE RIGHT PLACE

You don't need to have all the answers. You don't need to see the full map. You don't need to feel confident. What you need is to listen for His voice, obey His instruction, and stay in position, even when nothing makes sense.

Because when logic fails, God prevails. And what doesn't make sense to man will always make glory for God.

PART I

THE CALL AND THE CONFUSION

CHAPTER 1

GOD CHOOSES THE LEAST LIKELY

GIDEON'S CALL AND OUR INSECURITY

Scripture Focus: Judges 6:11–16

Gideon was not a warrior. He wasn't a seasoned leader. He wasn't from a prestigious tribe. In fact, when we first meet him in Judges 6, he's hiding—threshing wheat in a winepress to avoid the Midianites. He was fearful, doubtful, and insecure. Yet, this is the man God chose to deliver Israel from oppression. Why? Because God doesn't choose based on human criteria—He chooses based on divine purpose.

GOD SEES DIFFERENTLY THAN MAN

When the angel of the Lord appeared to Gideon, He greeted him with a name that contradicted his current behavior: **"The Lord is with thee, thou mighty man of valour" (Judges 6:12 - KJV).** There was nothing valiant about hiding. But God wasn't speaking to who Gideon was in the moment—He was speaking to who Gideon would become by divine empowerment.

This is often God's pattern. He speaks your end while you're still at your beginning. He calls you by your destiny while you're still living in fear. He calls the unqualified and equips them later. Why? So that no flesh will glory in His presence (see 1 Corinthians 1:27–29).

THE CALL COMES IN OBSCURITY

God didn't call Gideon on a battlefield. He called him in secret, in solitude, and in hiding. Sometimes your greatest call comes in seasons of isolation when no one sees you, when you feel like you're the last option, when life has silenced your confidence; yet, it's in those places that God's voice becomes clearest.

"But God hath chosen the foolish things of the world to confound the wise..." —1 Corinthians 1:27 (KJV)

INSECURITY IS NOT A DISQUALIFICATION

Gideon's first response to the call was self-doubt:

"my family is poor in Manasseh, and I am the least in my father's house." (Judges 6:15 - KJV)

Sound familiar?

Many of us disqualify ourselves from divine assignments because of how we see ourselves. But God's strategy doesn't rely on your résumé. It's rooted in His sovereignty. Your insecurity might be the very thing that makes you usable because it makes you dependent on Him.

GOD'S STRATEGY REQUIRES SURRENDER

The superior strategy of God often starts with surrender, not strength. God doesn't need your ability; He desires your availability. He wants your "yes," even when you feel unworthy. Gideon's journey began not with courage, but with conversation—with God telling him, **"Surely I will be with thee" (Judges 6:16 - KJV).**

REFLECTION QUESTIONS

1. What excuses have you given God that reflect Gideon's insecurity?

2. Can you identify a time when God called you while you were in hiding?

3. How can you surrender your fear and inadequacy to God today?

DECLARATION

I declare that God's call on my life is greater than my insecurity. I am chosen, not because I am strong, but because He is with me. I am who He says I am—mighty, purposed, and equipped for victory. I reject the lie that I am too weak, too small, or too late. God's strategy includes me!

PRAYER

Father, thank You for seeing more in me than I see in myself. Like Gideon, I often feel inadequate and hidden. Yet You call me by my future, not my failure. Help me to say yes to You, even when I don't understand the fullness of Your plan. Teach me to trust that Your strategy is always superior, even when it doesn't make sense to me. Use me for Your glory. In Jesus' name. Amen.

CHAPTER 2

TEARING DOWN THE ALTARS

BEFORE GOD CAN BUILD, HE MUST FIRST BREAK

Scripture Focus: Judges 6:25–32

After Gideon accepted the call of God, the very next instruction was not to fight a battle but to confront the idolatry in his own household. Before God would allow Gideon to defeat the Midianites, He required him to tear down the altar of Baal and the Asherah pole beside it. This chapter reveals a profound spiritual truth: God cannot build His strategy upon contaminated ground. Before there is elevation, there must be purification.

THE ALTARS IN YOUR OWN BACKYARD

Judges 6:25 says, **"Take thy father's young bullock, even the second bullock of seven years old, and throw down the altar of Baal that thy father hath, and cut down the grove that is by it:"** **(KJV).**

This wasn't a pagan temple in a foreign land—it was in Gideon's father's yard. The idolatry was close, familiar, and accepted by the community. Yet God required Gideon to address what had become normalized. Why? Because you cannot war for God publicly if you won't war against sin privately.

Before we can lead spiritual revolutions, we must experience personal reformation. What altars in your life—pride, fear, people-pleasing, self-reliance—must be torn down to make room for God's strategy?

REVIVAL REQUIRES CONFRONTATION

God's strategy often demands courage, not just to face enemies, but to confront culture. Gideon had to risk reputation, family ties, and personal safety to obey God's instruction. The strategy of heaven will sometimes offend the traditions of earth. But revival doesn't begin with applause; it begins with repentance.

Gideon obeyed, but he did it at night (see Judges 6:27), not because he lacked faith, but because he feared the backlash. God still honored the obedience. Boldness often grows in the process. Start with obedience, and boldness will follow.

THE COST OF OBEDIENCE

When the townspeople saw that the altar was destroyed, they wanted Gideon executed (see Judges 6:30). Choosing God's way will often make you misunderstood, even by those closest to you. But Joash, Gideon's father, surprisingly defended him, saying,

> **"Will ye plead for Baal? will ye save him? he that will plead for him, let him be put to death whilst it is yet morning: if he be a god, let him plead for himself, because one hath cast down his altar." (Judges 6:31 - KJV).**

When you take a stand for righteousness, God will raise unexpected allies to defend your obedience. You are never alone when you are in God's will.

GOD WILL NOT SHARE HIS GLORY

Why did the altar need to come down before the army could rise? Because God will not share His glory with another (see Isaiah 42:8). His strategy for victory will never be mixed with idols, distractions, or divided allegiance. If God is going to use you to tear down spiritual strongholds, you must first tear down compromise in your own camp.

God's strategy begins with consecration.

REFLECTION QUESTIONS

1. Are there any "altars" in your life that God is asking you to tear down?

2. Is there an area of obedience you've delayed because of fear or pressure from others?

3. What would spiritual reformation look like in your own household?

DECLARATION

I declare that I will no longer tolerate altars in my life that compete with God's authority. I tear down every idol of compromise, fear, tradition, and sin. My obedience is complete, and my altar is pure. I stand for truth, even when it costs me comfort. The ground of my heart belongs fully to God, and I am ready for His strategy to be fulfilled in me.

PRAYER

Lord, search me and expose every altar that dishonors You. Give me the courage to tear down what is familiar but sinful. I don't want to mix the holy with the profane. Make me a vessel of purity and obedience. Help me to stand for righteousness, even if it causes discomfort or criticism. Let Your fire fall on a clean altar. In Jesus' name. Amen.

CHAPTER 3

THE TEST OF TRUST

FLEECES, FEAR, AND FOLLOWING GOD ANYWAY

Scripture Focus: Judges 6:36–40

F ollowing God often brings us to a crossroads: *Will we trust His word or wait for further confirmation?* On Gideon's journey, we see a man who had answered the call, obeyed the first instruction, and now stands on the edge of a divine mission. But fear hadn't left him yet. His next move? A test of trust through a fleece.

Many criticize Gideon for asking God to confirm His will, but in truth, Gideon represents the human condition: we want to believe, but we also want to be sure. Trust is not proven in the absence of fear but in the presence of it.

THE FLEECE: A CRY FOR REASSURANCE

Judges 6:36–37 says, **"And Gideon said unto God, If thou wilt save Israel by mine hand, as thou hast said, behold, I will put a fleece of wool in the floor; and if the dew be on the fleece only, and it be dry upon all the earth beside, then shall I know that thou wilt save Israel by mine hand, as thou hast said." (KJV).**

Gideon wasn't asking for a sign because he was disobedient—he was asking for a sign because he wanted to obey with confidence. And God, in His mercy, honored the request, not once, but twice. This shows the patience of a God who understands our hesitations.

Sometimes, you don't need a different calling; you just need divine reassurance to walk boldly into what God already said.

GOD'S ASSURANCE DOESN'T EQUAL GOD'S APPROVAL OF DELAY

Though God answered Gideon's fleece request, He didn't stop the timeline of His strategy. Heaven's clock was still moving. Sometimes, we delay not because God hasn't spoken, but because we want 100% certainty before we take the first step. But faith is the substance of things hoped for, not things proven (see Hebrews 11:1).

God might meet you in your fear, but He won't let your fear lead the strategy. The test of trust isn't whether God speaks, it's whether you will move forward after He does.

TRUST IS GROWN THROUGH RELATIONSHIP

God didn't rebuke Gideon for asking twice. He responded to the fleece as a loving Father does to a hesitant child. This shows us that trust grows in the soil of relationship. The more we walk with God, the more we learn to take Him at His word without always needing extra signs.

Your current struggle to trust doesn't disqualify you. But it is a call to grow deeper in faith.

FOLLOWING GOD ANYWAY

At some point, the fleece must be folded up. The test must end. The step must be taken. God's strategy for victory cannot be delayed indefinitely because of our indecision. Gideon asked. God answered. And then it was time to move.

God may be confirming His word to you again and again, but eventually, He requires movement. The test of trust matures into action.

"Trust in the Lord with all thine heart; and lean not unto thine own understanding." —Proverbs 3:5

REFLECTION QUESTIONS

1. What area of your life are you still "putting out a fleece" over?

2. How has God already confirmed His direction to you?

3. What would it look like for you to take the next step, even if you're still afraid?

DECLARATION

I declare that I will trust God, even when I do not see the full picture. I will not remain stuck in indecision. My faith is growing. My ears are open to His voice. I reject the lie that I need more signs to move forward. I have God's promise, and that is enough. I walk by faith, not by sight.

PRAYER

Lord, thank You for being patient with me when I struggle to trust. Like Gideon, I sometimes ask for reassurance, not out of rebellion, but because I want to obey You confidently. Help me to know Your voice clearly. Strengthen my faith to step forward, even when I still feel afraid. May my trust in You deepen daily. In Jesus' name. Amen.

PART II

THE STRATEGY THAT DEFIES REASON

CHAPTER 4

TOO MANY MEN: THE POWER OF REDUCTION

WHEN LESS BECOMES MORE IN GOD'S HANDS

Scripture Focus: Judges 7:1–3

One of the most staggering moments in Gideon's story happens when God declares:

"The people who are with you are too many for Me to give the Midianites into their hands, lest Israel claim glory for itself…" (Judges 7:2 - NKJV).

What a contradiction! Human strategy says: the more the better. God's strategy? Reduce, so I can be revealed.

Sometimes, God's first step in fulfilling His promise is subtraction. He removes what we thought we needed so that when victory comes, we know exactly where the credit belongs.

WHEN STRENGTH BECOMES A STUMBLING BLOCK

Gideon had gathered 32,000 men—a decent army, especially compared to the vast number of Midianites. But God saw danger in the numbers, not danger of defeat but danger of pride. God was not just after a battle victory; He was after spiritual purification. He knew if the army were too large, Israel would boast, **"My own hand has saved me."**

God will often reduce your resources, options, and support so that when a breakthrough comes, the only explanation is that God did it.

THE FEARFUL MUST GO

God instructed Gideon to make a public announcement: **"Whoever is fearful and afraid, let him turn and depart…" (Judges 7:3 - NKJV).**

And 22,000 men left. More than two-thirds walked away.

Why? Because fear is contagious. God was about to birth a miracle, and fear couldn't be in the room. When God is preparing to release His strategy through you, He will intentionally separate you from people whose fear will interfere with faith.

Let them go.

LESS IS THE SETUP FOR MORE

God reduced Gideon's army, not to punish him but to position him. In God's strategy, reduction is often preparation for supernatural results.

When you feel like you're losing people, opportunities, or influence, remember: *God's subtraction is often a setup for His glory to be multiplied.*

"Except a corn of wheat fall into the ground and die, it abideth alone: but if it die, it bringeth forth much fruit." — **John 12:24 (KJV)**

REFLECTION QUESTIONS

1. What has God removed from your life recently that initially felt like a loss?

2. Are there people in your circle who are operating in fear rather than faith?

3. How have you seen God work through a season of "less"?

DECLARATION

I declare that reduction in my life is not rejection—it is redirection. God is preparing me for greater glory. I release the need to rely on numbers, validation, or support. My confidence is in the Lord. Every subtraction is a divine strategy for supernatural success.

PRAYER

Father, thank You for Your wisdom that surpasses mine. Help me to trust You when You reduce what I thought I needed. Remove anything from my life that would cause me to rely on myself instead of You. Let my dependence grow deeper so that You alone get the glory. In Jesus' name. Amen.

CHAPTER 5

THE FINAL 300: PURGING FOR PURPOSE

GOD ONLY NEEDS WHAT'S ALIGNED WITH HIM

Scripture Focus: Judges 7:4–8

J ust when Gideon might've thought, Okay, 10,000 is still manageable, God speaks again: **"The people are yet too many..."** (Judges 7:4 - KJV).

God then leads Gideon to a second test—this one far more specific. Only 300 men remained after this test. Why? Because victory in God's plan isn't based on quantity but quality—on alignment, not appearance.

THE WATER TEST: A TEST OF DISCERNMENT AND READINESS

God told Gideon to watch how the men drank water. Those who cupped the water and lapped it like a dog—remaining alert—were chosen. Those who knelt down to drink in a more relaxed posture were sent home.

This was not about thirst; it was about vigilance. God's final army needed to be watchful, prepared, and spiritually discerning.

In this hour, God is separating those who are casual from those who are committed—those who are distracted from those who are disciplined.

THE POWER OF ALIGNMENT

God doesn't need crowds—He needs carriers of His vision. The 300 represented those who were postured for purpose. Alignment matters more than appearance. Not everyone who follows you is fit for the fight you're about to face.

In God's superior strategy, less is not weak—less is lean, focused, obedient, and God-chosen.

GOD IS NARROWING YOUR CIRCLE

This final selection wasn't random. It was divine refinement. When God begins to reduce your circle to the faithful few, don't mourn. Rejoice. He's surrounding you with warriors, not spectators.

Every person in your life should be tested by the water—by how they drink, by how they prepare, by how they posture themselves when no one is watching.

"Can two walk together, except they be agreed?" —Amos 3:3 (KJV)

REFLECTION QUESTIONS

1. Are you in alignment with God's strategy, or are you simply "present" but unprepared?

2. Who around you passes the "water test"—those who stay alert and focused?

3. What is God teaching you about quality over quantity in this season?

DECLARATION

I declare that I am in divine alignment. I am part of God's faithful few. I am vigilant, watchful, and prepared. I am not distracted. I am focused on the mission and walking with those who carry the same burden. God's victory will come through my obedience and spiritual readiness.

PRAYER

Lord, thank You for refining my circle and positioning me for purpose. Help me to remain alert in the spirit and focused on Your will. Remove anything in my life that causes distraction or disobedience. Surround me with the committed—not the casual—and use me for Your glory. In Jesus' name. Amen.

CHAPTER 6

WEAPONS THAT MAKE NO SENSE

TRUMPETS, JARS, AND TORCHES IN BATTLE?

Scripture Focus: Judges 7:16–22

It's one thing for God to reduce your army. It's another thing for Him to hand you a battle plan that looks more like a worship service than a war strategy. In Judges 7:16–18, Gideon divides his 300 men into three companies and places in their hands—not swords or spears—but trumpets, empty pitchers, and torches.

No commander in history would equip warriors with jars and lamps to face an enemy that outnumbered them by the thousands. But here lies the mystery of divine strategy: God doesn't need what the world considers strong—He needs what is surrendered.

When God gives you weapons that make no sense, it's because He's about to get a victory that makes no sense.

UNUSUAL WEAPONS, UNEXPLAINABLE VICTORY

The weapons God chooses reflect His nature: unconventional, unpredictable, and unmatched. In this story, trumpets would announce, jars would break, and torches would blaze—all under the cover of night. It wasn't logical. It wasn't comfortable. But it was divinely orchestrated.

God intentionally gives us tools that defy human logic to ensure He receives all the glory. He wants to defeat spiritual enemies with strategies that cannot be explained by intellect, education, connections, or human effort.

SOUND, BROKENNESS, AND LIGHT: A PROPHETIC PATTERN

Let's look at the weapons symbolically:

- **Trumpets (Sound):** The trumpet was a signal of war and a declaration of authority. In the spirit, sound represents worship, intercession, and prophetic declaration. When we lift our voices in obedience, God moves.

- **Empty Jars (Brokenness):** These clay jars had to be shattered for the light to shine through. This symbolizes our own brokenness. We are vessels of clay (see 2 Corinthians 4:7), and it is only when we are broken before God that His light is revealed through us.

- **Torches (Light):** The torch hidden inside the jar represents the fire of God within you. But the fire won't be seen until the vessel breaks. Revival often follows brokenness.

This isn't just a military tactic—it's a prophetic picture of how God uses worship, surrender, and spiritual illumination to bring about victory.

OBEDIENCE IN THE FACE OF RIDICULE

Imagine being one of the 300. You've already seen thousands walk away. Now your leader hands you a horn, a jar, and a flame. You might feel embarrassed, ill-equipped, or exposed. But obedience requires trusting the voice of God over the threat of the enemy.

Gideon's men didn't argue. They didn't substitute God's plan with something "more logical." They followed the strategy exactly—and that obedience unleashed supernatural terror in the enemy's camp.

"And the three hundred blew the trumpets, and the Lord set every man's sword against his fellow, even throughout all the host: and the host fled to Bethshittah in Zererath, and to the border of Abelmeholah, unto Tabbath." — Judges 7:22 (KJV)

Notice: the enemy turned on themselves. You won't even have to lift a sword when you fully walk in divine strategy.

GOD WILL USE WHAT DOESN'T MAKE SENSE

Have you ever felt like what God gave you wasn't enough?

Like you were showing up to a war with a worship song, a broken heart, and a flicker of faith?

Good. That's exactly how God operates. He specializes in using what the world laughs at to release heaven's power. If God handed you a trumpet, a torch, and a jar, then that's what will work.

WHEN GOD ANOINTS WHAT YOU ALREADY HAVE

Too many times we pray for new weapons when God has already equipped us. He just wants to anoint what's already in our hands. The trumpet, the jar, and the torch didn't look like weapons—until God breathed on them.

What if your praise is your weapon? What if your brokenness is your qualification? What if your fire is enough?

You don't need to fight like the world to win the battle. You just need to follow the strategy of heaven.

REFLECTION QUESTIONS

1. What "weapons" has God placed in your hands that seem illogical to others?

2. Are you willing to obey, even when His instructions don't make sense to you?

3. In what ways has brokenness in your life revealed God's glory?

DECLARATION

I declare that I will follow God's strategy, even when it defies human reason. My worship is my weapon. My brokenness will not disqualify me—it will reveal His light. I will not fear the unconventional methods of God, for He is fighting for me. My victory will be unexplainable but undeniable. I am equipped. I am aligned. I am ready.

PRAYER

Lord, thank You for the strategy that confounds the wise. Help me to trust the weapons You've given me, even when they don't make sense. Let my sound be bold, my surrender be complete, and my fire shine bright. Break everything in me that conceals Your glory, and use my life as a testimony that You are the God who wins in ways man cannot predict. In Jesus' name. Amen.

PART III

THE VICTORY THAT GLORIFIES GOD

CHAPTER 7

SURROUNDED BUT EMPOWERED

HOW GOD USES UNUSUAL POSITIONING

Scripture Focus: Judges 7:19–21

There is a unique kind of fear that strikes the heart when you realize you're outnumbered—when the odds seem stacked against you; when you look around and see no way of escape. Gideon and his 300 men knew what that felt like. Surrounded by tens of thousands of Midianites, Amalekites, and **"all the people of the East,"** they were strategically positioned around the enemy camp with nothing but trumpets, jars, and torches.

From a natural perspective, they were vulnerable. Exposed. Outmatched.

But from God's perspective, they were exactly where they needed to be.

Because in divine strategy, it's not about who surrounds you—it's about Who sent you.

GOD USES THE SURROUNDED TO DELIVER THE SURPRISING

Judges 7:19a says, **"So Gideon, and the hundred men that were with him, came unto the outside of the camp in the beginning of the middle watch;" (KJV).**

This wasn't a random moment. It was the beginning of the middle watch—around midnight—when most soldiers would be at their weakest, tired or transitioning shifts. God intentionally chooses moments that man does not expect. He sends victory into the places that seem the darkest.

Even though Gideon's men were surrounded by enemies, they were surrounded by purpose first. Their very positioning was a setup for breakthrough.

OBEDIENCE IS GREATER THAN PROTECTION

Notice: God did not first give them protection; He gave them position.

This is where many of us struggle. We want God to insulate us before we obey Him. We want guarantees before we go. But God says, **"I'll cover you in the assignment, not apart from it."**

Gideon and his men were told to surround the camp. Not retreat from it. Not wait for backup. Surround the thing that's trying to intimidate you.

Your obedience may place you in vulnerable territory, but it also places you in the perfect position for divine empowerment.

THERE'S POWER IN UNITY AND TIMING

Judges 7:20 tells us: **"And the three companies blew the trumpets, and brake the pitchers, and held the lamps in their left hands, and the trumpets in their right hands to blow withal: and they cried, The sword of the Lord, and of Gideon." (KJV).**

All 300 acted at once. They didn't delay. They didn't wait to see who would go first. There was synchronized obedience. God's power often manifests when unity meets obedience in divine timing.

They didn't need a sword—they needed sound. They didn't need shields—they needed surrender. They didn't need thousands—they needed unity.

SURROUNDED DOESN'T MEAN DEFEATED

What if being surrounded is not a sign of defeat, but a signal for divine intervention?

Sometimes the enemy surrounds you, thinking he has the upper hand, only for God to flip the situation and use it for an ambush. That's what happened here. As Gideon's men surrounded the enemy and released their sound, confusion broke out among the enemy forces. The Midianites turned on each other.

"And the three hundred blew the trumpets, and the Lord set every man's sword against his fellow, even throughout all the host: and the host fled to Bethshittah in Zererath, and to the border of Abelmeholah, unto Tabbath." —Judges 7:22 (KJV).

God took the enemy's numbers and turned them into a liability. That's the God we serve. He makes your opposition destroy itself.

YOU'RE EMPOWERED BY WHAT'S IN YOU, NOT WHAT'S AROUND YOU

Gideon's men were not empowered because of their environment—they were empowered by what they carried: sound, fire, light, and obedience.

What if your real weapon isn't your surroundings, but your inner surrender to God's will?

You may be surrounded right now by financial pressure, emotional turmoil, family crises, or spiritual warfare. But like Gideon's army, you're not alone. You're empowered. You're positioned. You're obedient. And heaven is fighting for you.

REFLECTION QUESTIONS

1. What current situation in your life feels like you're surrounded?

2. How has God positioned you to trust Him, even when it seems risky?

3. Are you moving in unity with those God has called you to walk with?

DECLARATION

I declare that even when I am surrounded, I am not defeated. I am empowered by the Spirit of God. I am positioned for victory, not ruin. My obedience has placed me in the perfect place for divine results. I walk in unity, boldness, and timing. My enemies may surround me, but God surrounds them.

PRAYER

Father, I thank You for positioning me with purpose, even when I feel surrounded by pressure. Please help me to trust that my location in this battle is no accident. Empower me to obey fully, stand boldly, and move in unity with those You've aligned with me. Let Your presence be my protection, and Your glory be my reward. Surround me with Your fire, and use my life to confuse and defeat the plans of the enemy. In Jesus' name. Amen.

CHAPTER 8

BREAKING THE JAR: A SYMBOL OF SURRENDER

VICTORY COMES THROUGH BROKENNESS

Scripture Focus: Judges 7:19–20; 2 Corinthians 4:7

The sound of victory in Gideon's story wasn't just the trumpet blast, it was the shattering of jars. Each of the 300 men held a clay pitcher with a torch hidden inside, and at the appointed moment, they broke the jar. Only then could the fire inside shine out.

> **"And the three companies blew the trumpets, and brake the pitchers, and held the lamps in their left hands, and the trumpets in their right hands to blow withal: and they cried, The sword of the Lord, and of Gideon." —Judges 7:20 (KJV)**

This act was not just military; it was symbolic. It prophetically revealed a key spiritual principle: God's light is most visible in us when we allow ourselves to be broken.

In the kingdom of God, brokenness is not weakness—it is power. And the victory that confounds the enemy often flows through the vessel that's been shattered for God's glory.

WE CARRY TREASURE IN FRAGILE VESSELS

Paul writes in 2 Corinthians 4:7, **"But we have this treasure in earthen vessels, that the excellence of the power may be of God, and not of us." (KJV).**

You and I are like those clay jars—fragile, flawed, breakable. But inside us is a heavenly treasure—the light of Christ. And sometimes, God allows the vessel to be broken so that the glory within can finally shine out.

That's why your "breaking" wasn't a punishment, it was preparation. What felt like loss was God making space for light to break through.

THE HIDDEN FIRE CAN'T STAY HIDDEN

Before the jar was broken, the torch remained concealed. It's not that the fire didn't exist—it just wasn't visible. There are many believers who have fire on the inside, but pride, fear, shame, or self-preservation keep that fire trapped within a hard shell.

God's strategy for Gideon required that the torch be seen. But visibility required vulnerability.

The fire in you won't impact the world until the outer shell is surrendered and shattered.

THE PURPOSE OF BREAKING IS REVELATION, NOT DESTRUCTION

God never breaks for the sake of pain—He breaks for the sake of purpose.

Gideon's army didn't break their jars at random. They broke them at the exact moment God instructed, right after the trumpet sounded. There's timing, even in your breaking. What may feel like devastation may actually be divine orchestration.

God is saying: **"I'm breaking you so that what I placed in you can shine without resistance."**

THE SOUND OF SURRENDER IS LOUDER THAN THE SOUND OF STRATEGY

When the jars were shattered, it created a violent, echoing sound in the night. To the enemy camp, it was terrifying. Imagine hundreds of clay vessels exploding in unison, combined with the blast of trumpets and cries of war. It sounded like chaos, but it was surrender.

The enemy doesn't know what to do with someone who is fully surrendered to God.

When you break before the Lord, it sends a shockwave into the spirit realm. The enemy knows that a person who is no longer trying to protect their image or cling to control is unstoppable in the hands of God.

YOUR BREAKING IS A WEAPON

Yes, your brokenness is part of God's plan. Not to leave you shattered, but to shine His glory through you.

Gideon didn't fight with weapons in the traditional sense. He fought with obedience, sound, fire, and brokenness. And the enemy fell apart.

You don't need to be perfect, polished, or put together. You just need to be breakable in the hands of the Master.

"The sacrifices of God are a broken spirit: a broken and a contrite heart, O God, thou wilt not despise." —Psalm 51:17 (KJV).

REFLECTION QUESTIONS

1. What areas of your life have recently experienced breaking?

2. Have you been trying to hide your light behind a shell of self-protection or fear?

3. How has God used your brokenness to reach others?

DECLARATION

I declare that my breaking is not my ending, it is my birthing. The light of God within me will no longer be hidden. I am surrendered. I am vulnerable. I am usable. The cracks in my life are the places where His fire shines brightest. I am a vessel of His glory, and even in brokenness, I carry power.

PRAYER

Father, I surrender every part of me, especially the pieces I've tried to keep whole for the sake of pride, image, or self-preservation. Break me in the areas that are hindering Your light. Let my brokenness become a testimony of Your power. I no longer resist the process. Use every crack, every scar, every part of me for Your glory. Shine through me until darkness trembles. In Jesus' name. Amen.

CHAPTER 9

THE BATTLE BELONGS TO THE LORD

HOW OBEDIENCE BRINGS SUPERNATURAL RESULTS

Scripture Focus: Judges 7:21–22, 2 Chronicles 20:15, Exodus 14:14

There is something utterly powerful and humbling about watching God move in a situation that you know you couldn't have fixed on your own. After the trumpet sounded, the jars shattered, and the torches blazed, Gideon's men stood in position but they didn't have to lift a sword. God did the fighting.

Judges 7:21 says, **"And they stood every man in his place round about the camp; and all the host ran, and cried, and fled." (KJV).**

What a profound truth: *The battle was won, not by force, but by obedience.*

There is a point in every believer's journey where they must come to terms with this reality: *the battle belongs to the Lord.* We are not called to figure it all out—we are called to trust, obey, and stand in position.

STANDING STILL CAN BE SPIRITUAL WARFARE

Gideon's army didn't charge forward. They didn't chase the Midianites. They simply stood. And in their standing, God caused confusion in the enemy's camp. The Midianites began to fight each other. God turned their unity into chaos, their confidence into fear and their strength into weakness.

This is not the first time God has fought on behalf of His people:

- In Exodus 14:14, God said to Moses, **"The Lord shall fight for you, and ye shall hold your peace." (KJV).**

- In 2 Chronicles 20:15, God told Jehoshaphat, **"Be not afraid nor dismayed by reason of this great multitude; for the battle is not yours, but God's." (KJV).**

When you stop striving and start trusting, God steps in as your Defender.

OBEDIENCE UNLOCKS DIVINE POWER

It would have made more sense to gather weapons or come up with an escape route. But Gideon followed God's precise instruction, even when it sounded absurd. The power didn't come from their ability; it came from their obedience.

We often think victory depends on how hard we fight. But in the kingdom of God, victory is tied to obedience more than effort. Your job is to follow. His job is to fight.

When you obey God in the small details—when you speak when He says speak, stand when He says stand, stay when He says stay—He moves in ways you never imagined.

GOD LOVES TO FIGHT FOR THE UNDERDOG

Gideon's 300 versus the countless Midianites? That's no contest unless God is in the middle of it.

God consistently chooses the weak, the under-resourced, the outnumbered, and the overlooked to demonstrate His strength. He loves to set the stage so that when the victory comes, there is no doubt about where it came from.

> **"Not by might, nor by power, but by My Spirit, saith the Lord of hosts." —Zechariah 4:6 (KJV)**

YOUR POSITION DETERMINES THE OUTCOME

Judges 7:21 again emphasizes: **"And they stood every man in his place round about the camp; and all the host ran, and cried, and fled." (KJV).**

The battle wasn't won because they moved, it was won because they remained where they were assigned. Your position in the will of God is your protection.

Sometimes we lose battles, not because we weren't strong enough, but because we stepped out of place. Spiritual alignment matters. The safest place to be is in the center of God's strategy, even when everything around you says "move, panic, or retreat."

HE GETS THE GLORY

Why did God orchestrate the battle this way?

Because if Gideon had won with 32,000 men, they would have taken the credit. But with only 300 men, torches, jars, and trumpets, there's no mistaking who deserves the glory.

When God gives you a victory that you couldn't possibly earn or explain, it becomes a testimony of His supremacy and a beacon of faith for others.

Sometimes, God will delay a breakthrough until you let go of your own strategies, so He alone can get the glory.

REFLECTION QUESTIONS

1. Are there areas in your life where you're still trying to fight in your own strength?

2. What does it look like for you to "stand in your place" right now?

3. How has obedience positioned you for victories in past seasons?

DECLARATION

I declare that the battle belongs to the Lord. I will not fear, I will not strive, I will not retreat. I stand firm in obedience, knowing that my God fights for me. Every enemy of my purpose is defeated, not by my strength, but by the power of His hand. I trust God's plan, I honor His timing, and I give Him all the glory.

PRAYER

Lord, I surrender every battle I've been trying to fight in my own strength. Teach me to trust You deeply. Please help me to remain in position, even when I feel outnumbered or overwhelmed. I declare today that the battle belongs to You. Let Your power be revealed in my stillness, in my faith, and in my obedience. Win through me, Lord—for Your glory and for the good of others. In Jesus' name. Amen.

PART IV

APPLYING THE STRATEGY TO YOUR LIFE

CHAPTER 10

WHEN GOD DOESN'T MAKE SENSE BUT HE'S STILL RIGHT

TRUSTING DIVINE INSTRUCTION IN CONFUSING TIMES

Scripture Focus: Isaiah 55:8–9, Proverbs 3:5–6, Hebrews 11:1

L et's be honest: *sometimes God's ways simply do not make sense to the human mind.*

— Why would He reduce an army from 32,000 to 300?

— Why would He send men into battle with jars and torches instead of swords?

— Why would He call a fearful, insecure man like Gideon to lead the charge?

Because God doesn't operate according to our logic—He operates according to His sovereignty.

67

His strategies are not based on human understanding but on divine outcomes. And if we're going to walk with Him, we must learn to trust Him, even when nothing adds up.

GOD IS NOT CONFINED TO HUMAN LOGIC

Isaiah 55:8–9 reminds us: **"For my thoughts are not your thoughts, neither are your ways my ways," saith the Lord. "For as the heavens are higher than the earth, so are my ways higher than your ways, and my thoughts than your thoughts." (KJV).**

We serve a God whose strategies transcend systems, human reasoning, and natural patterns. What seems foolish to man is often the very vehicle of breakthrough in God's hands.

— It didn't make sense when Noah built an ark in a world that had never seen rain.

— It didn't make sense when Moses stretched out a staff over the Red Sea.

— It didn't make sense when David faced Goliath with a sling and a stone.

But every time God gave an unusual instruction, obedience opened the door to a supernatural result.

YOU DON'T HAVE TO UNDERSTAND TO OBEY

One of the greatest tests of faith is following a God you don't always understand. Trusting a plan you didn't write. Walking into places you never imagined.

"Trust in the Lord with all thine heart; and lean not unto thine own understanding. In all thy ways acknowledge him, and he shall direct thy paths." —Proverbs 3:5–6 (KJV)

Too often, we try to figure God out before we follow Him. But trust isn't built on explanations, it's built on relationship.

Gideon could've backed out at any stage. He could've said, **"This is too risky, too strange, too unreasonable."** But he chose to trust, even when God's strategy didn't make sense.

And that is the essence of faith.

"Now faith is the substance of things hoped for, the evidence of things not seen." —Hebrews 11:1 (KJV)

FAITH WALKS FORWARD WHILE QUESTIONS REMAIN

It's okay to have questions. Gideon had plenty:

- "Why has all this happened to us?" (see Judges 6:13).

- "How can I save Israel?" (see Judges 6:15).

- "If You are with me, show me a sign..." (see Judges 6:17).

But even in his questioning, he didn't stop moving.

Faith doesn't eliminate questions; it refuses to let questions become paralysis. Trust is choosing obedience while holding unanswered whys in your heart.

THERE'S PURPOSE IN THE PERPLEXITY

God's unusual methods often produce uncommon results. The confusion is not an accident—it's intentional. Why?

- To develop your dependence.
- To mature your discernment.
- To reveal His sovereignty.
- To remove your reliance on flesh.

God's strategy rarely makes sense at the start, but it always proves right in the end.

"Being confident of this very thing, that he which hath begun a good work in you will perform it until the day of Jesus Christ:" —Philippians 1:6 (KJV)

He doesn't begin a journey without having the ending fully secured.

IF YOU WAIT FOR IT TO MAKE SENSE, YOU'LL MISS IT

Miracles are usually wrapped in mystery.

If Gideon had waited for the strategy to "make sense," he would've missed the moment. If you demand clarity before obedience, you'll forfeit opportunities for God to show His glory.

Sometimes, God hides the full picture so that your obedience is pure. You obey, not because you see but because you believe.

GOD IS STILL RIGHT, EVEN WHEN IT FEELS WRONG

There are moments when God's direction feels backwards, risky, even unfair. But time always reveals that He was right all along.

- His delay is not denial.
- His silence is not absence.
- His restriction is not punishment.
- His confusion is not cruelty.

What doesn't make sense now will make purpose later.

And when the dust settles, you'll find yourself standing in a place that your logic could never have taken you, but obedience did.

REFLECTION QUESTIONS

1. Have you ever delayed obedience because you didn't understand God's instruction?

2. What area of your life is currently confusing but requires trust?

3. Can you look back and recall moments when God's strange strategies worked for your good?

DECLARATION

I declare that God's ways are higher than mine. I will not wait for clarity before I obey. I trust Him in confusion. I follow Him in faith. I walk in alignment, even when the road makes no sense. I declare that every divine instruction—even when strange—will lead to supernatural results in my life. God is not obligated to make sense, but He is always faithful.

PRAYER

Lord, I surrender the need to understand everything. Teach me to trust You deeply, even when nothing makes sense. Forgive me for the times I've delayed obedience waiting for clarity. Help me to remember that You are right, even when life feels wrong. Strengthen my faith to walk forward, even in mystery. I believe You, I trust You, and I follow You. In Jesus' name. Amen.

CHAPTER 11

YOUR 300 MOMENT: EMBRACING THE UNCONVENTIONAL

GOD'S WAY WILL ALWAYS WORK—EVEN WHEN IT LOOKS IMPOSSIBLE

Scripture Focus: Judges 7:7, Romans 8:31, 1 Corinthians 1:27–29

There comes a point in every believer's journey where God gives them what I call a "300 moment"—a defining season when He removes the familiar, reduces the numbers, defies the norm, and asks for full trust in His unconventional strategy.

For Gideon, that moment came when God said, **"By the three hundred men that lapped will I save you…" (Judges 7:7 - KJV).**

Can you imagine hearing that? You just watched 31,700 men walk away. You're left with less than 1% of what you started with. And then God says, **"This is enough."**

Everything in your flesh wants to resist. Logic screams, *"This isn't wise."* But your spirit senses something holy. God is about to show you what He can do with less—if it's surrendered.

YOUR "300 MOMENT" IS WHEN GOD ASKS YOU TO TRUST WHAT DOESN'T FEEL SAFE

Sometimes we say we trust God, but only when His plan agrees with our comfort zone.

Gideon's "300 moment" stripped away his safety net. His backup plan. His human strength. There was no plan B—just obedience to a God who had already seen the outcome.

"If God be for us, who can be against us?" —Romans 8:31 (KJV)

Your "300 moment" will often come right before your greatest victory, but it will require your full surrender, your willingness to stand with less, go with few or believe with nothing in sight.

WHEN GOD SHRINKS IT TO SHOW YOU IT'S HIM

God told Gideon directly: **"The people that are with thee are too many for me to give the Midianites into their hands, lest Israel vaunt themselves against me, saying, Mine own hand hath saved me." (Judges 7:2 - KJV).**

God is fiercely protective of His glory. He will allow things to shrink, scatter, or stop, not because He's punishing you, but because He's positioning the outcome so He alone gets the credit.

When the crowd leaves, when the support fades, when the budget gets cut, when the doors close—don't panic. It might be your "300 moment." And when that moment comes, you must choose: *panic or purpose?*

WHAT FEELS LIKE A SETBACK IS OFTEN DIVINE STRATEGY

Imagine standing on the battlefield with only 300 men, watching an army so vast it looks like "locusts" (see Judges 7:12). It doesn't look like strategy—it looks like sabotage.

But this is how God works. He creates a situation so impossible that when the victory comes, there's no other explanation but Him.

This is the God who:

- Shut the mouths of lions through a praying prophet (see Daniel 6).

- Opened a sea using a shepherd's staff (see Exodus 14).

- Resurrected the dead using nothing but a voice (see John 11).

He doesn't need what you think you need. He just needs you—available, obedient, and surrendered.

THIS IS WHERE FAITH GETS REAL

Your "300 moment" is the point where faith stops being theory and becomes practice. It's where you go:

- From saying "God provides" to trusting Him with no backup plan.

- From believing in "God's timing" to waiting while others pass you by.

- From quoting "God's ways are higher" to living without full understanding.

This is the stretch. This is the place where character is forged, identity is clarified, and power is released because God does His best work with the remnant.

GOD USES THE UNCONVENTIONAL TO PRODUCE THE UNCOMMON

1 Corinthians 1:27–29 reminds us: **"But God has chosen the foolish things of the world to confound the wise... that no flesh should glory in His presence."**

God's way is rarely conventional. He chooses:

- A barren woman to birth a prophet (Hannah).
- A young shepherd to defeat a giant (David).
- A teenage virgin to carry the Savior (Mary).
- A broken army of 300 to deliver a nation (Gideon).

If what you're facing feels unqualified, unexpected, or unconventional, you might be exactly where God wants you.

DON'T DISMISS THE POWER IN THE FEW

Many believers miss their "300 moment" because they chase crowds, affirmation, or visible strength.

But God never needs the majority to do a miracle. He works powerfully with the available minority. In fact, many great revivals, breakthroughs, and kingdom movements started with:

- A remnant
- A whisper
- A yes

Your "300 moment" is a reminder that less doesn't mean lacking. It means you've entered the realm of the miraculous.

REFLECTION QUESTIONS

1. Are you in a season where God has reduced or stripped something in your life?

2. What does your current "300 moment" look like?

3. Are you willing to obey God, even when the method looks unconventional or risky?

DECLARATION

I declare that my "300 moment" is not a sign of weakness—it is proof that God is about to move. I will not panic when God reduces. I will not retreat when others walk away. I am aligned with His plan, even when I don't understand it. The few in my life are enough because God is with me. I am positioned for victory through divine strategy.

PRAYER

Lord, I surrender to Your strategy, even when it feels uncomfortable or confusing. I release my grip on what makes me feel secure and choose to trust Your perfect plan. Teach me to stand boldly in my "300 moment." Remind me that You are my Defender, my Source, and my Victory. Use what's left in my life to bring about supernatural results. I trust You. I honor You. I follow You. In Jesus' name. Amen.

CHAPTER 12

VICTORY WITHOUT A SWORD

WINNING SPIRITUAL BATTLES GOD'S WAY

Scripture Focus: Judges 7:20–22, Ephesians 6:10–17, Zechariah 4:6

The final act of Gideon's story in Judges 7 is perhaps the most shocking of all, not just because of the overwhelming victory, but because not one sword was lifted by Israel's hand in combat. They surrounded the camp, obeyed the strange strategy, blew the trumpets, shattered the jars, raised the torches, and cried out: **"The sword of the Lord, and of Gideon!" —Judges 7:20 (KJV)**

But here's the paradox: *they spoke of a sword, but never actually wielded one.*

The battle was won without physical weapons because when God fights for you, obedience becomes your warfare, and faith becomes your blade.

THE SWORD THAT WAS NEVER DRAWN

We never read that Gideon or his 300 warriors used swords to strike down the Midianites. Instead, the Bible says: **"And the three hundred blew the trumpets, and the Lord set every man's sword against his fellow, even throughout all the host: and the host fled to Bethshittah in Zererath, and to the border of Abelmeholah, unto Tabbath."** —Judges 7:22 (KJV)

It was the enemy's own swords that turned on each other. This victory wasn't about might. It wasn't about manpower. It wasn't about military advantage. It was about God showing that His strategy works without natural intervention.

THIS BATTLE WAS WON IN THE SPIRIT FIRST

Everything that happened in Gideon's victory mirrors a spiritual principle: battles are won in the unseen before they are manifested in the seen.

— The trumpets represent worship and sound—**spiritual authority**.
— The breaking jars represent surrender—**spiritual sacrifice**.
— The torches represent light—**spiritual truth and revelation**.
— The cry, "The sword of the Lord," represents a spoken word—**prophetic declaration**.

Together, these formed a spiritual ambush that caused panic, confusion, and ultimately the collapse of a superior enemy.

The same is true today. We do not fight with swords and spears— we fight with: **"the sword of the Spirit, which is the word of God." —Ephesians 6:17 (KJV)**

WARFARE THAT DOESN'T LOOK LIKE WARFARE

One of the reasons God's strategy confounds us is that His methods often don't resemble a battle at all.

— Praise instead of panic.
— Silence instead of retaliation.
— Prayer instead of arguing.
— Fasting instead of fighting.
— Stillness instead of striving.

This is supernatural warfare and it is far more powerful than human resistance.

The Israelites could not have planned a victory like this. No general could have written this tactic. It was born out of heaven, and it worked. Because when you follow God's unconventional strategy, you will get undeniable results.

THE SWORD OF THE LORD IS IN HIS WORD

When Gideon and his men cried, **"The sword of the Lord and of Gideon!"** they were declaring alignment. They weren't fighting in their own name or power—they were under God's authority.

Your greatest weapon is not your resources, connections, or intellect. It is the Word of God. Every lie of the enemy, every fear, every demonic assignment is broken when the Word is declared boldly.

The enemy is not afraid of your talent. He is afraid of truth. When you declare scripture in faith, you are drawing the most powerful sword in existence.

> **"For the word of God is quick, and powerful, and sharper than any twoedged sword…" —Hebrews 4:12 (KJV)**

WHAT YOU DON'T USE IN THE FLESH, GOD WILL MULTIPLY IN THE SPIRIT

Sometimes God will intentionally remove what you think you need (like a sword) just to prove that He is your victory.

You may feel under-equipped. You may feel like you're going into battle with nothing but a trumpet and a prayer. But that's when heaven gets involved. That's when angels are released. That's when the enemy starts to tremble, not because of what you carry, but because of Who sent you.

> **Not by might, nor by power, but by my spirit, saith the Lord of hosts. —Zechariah 4:6 (KJV)**

VICTORY THAT CAN'T BE EXPLAINED, ONLY WITNESSED

Gideon's victory spread beyond the battlefield. When the surrounding tribes heard what had happened, they came to assist in finishing the defeat. News spread fast because when God gives you a supernatural victory, people will see it, and they'll want to be part of what God is doing.

Let this truth settle deep in your heart: the battles you win in the spirit will shift things in the natural.

REFLECTION QUESTIONS

1. Have you been relying on physical or natural methods instead of spiritual weapons?

2. What battle in your life requires a surrender to God's unconventional warfare?

3. How can you begin to use "the sword of the Spirit"— God's Word—more intentionally?

DECLARATION

I declare that I will win battles God's way. I will not lean on human strength, natural weapons, or logical plans. My sword is the Word of God. My weapon is obedience. My power comes from the Spirit. I trust God's method, even when it's unconventional. I am victorious, not because of what I carry in my hand, but because of who I follow with my heart.

PRAYER

Lord, thank You for reminding me that the battle belongs to You. Teach me how to war in the Spirit with prayer, worship, Your Word, and total surrender. I lay down my sword so You can lift up Yours. Fight through me. Win through me. And may every victory in my life bring glory to Your name. In Jesus' name. Amen.

CONCLUSION

THE SUPERIOR STRATEGY ALWAYS BELONGS TO GOD

Scripture Focus: Proverbs 19:21, Psalm 33:10–11, Isaiah 14:24

LOOKING BACK TO SEE CLEARLY

As we reflect on Gideon's journey—his call, his fear, the reduction of his army, the strange weapons, and the supernatural victory—one truth rises above them all: *God's strategy is always superior.* Not occasionally. Not when the odds are favorable. Not when things go as planned. Always.

Even when it looks backward. Even when it feels risky. Even when it seems like God is doing the exact opposite of what you prayed for, He knows exactly what He's doing.

WHAT THIS JOURNEY HAS TAUGHT US

From Judges 6–7, we've learned some transformational principles:

- **God calls the unlikely:** He doesn't choose based on status, strength, or appearance—He chooses based on availability and destiny.

85

- **Before victory comes consecration:** You cannot bring down strongholds until you first tear down altars in your own life.

- **Obedience is the hinge of God's power:** When we follow His specific instructions, no matter how small or strange, heaven responds.

- **Reduction is often preparation:** God removes excess, not to punish you, but to purify the path ahead so that He alone may receive the glory.

- **Brokenness reveals the glory within:** We carry treasure in clay jars, and when we're broken before God, His light is revealed through us.

- **Stillness can be warfare:** Sometimes God's strategy is not to fight harder, but to stand firmer.

- **Victory doesn't require a sword:** God's Word, your worship, and your obedience are greater weapons than any earthly resource.

YOUR LIFE, LIKE GIDEON'S, IS A TESTAMENT TO GOD'S STRATEGY

You've likely had your own Gideon moments. Maybe you're living in one right now.

— You've felt unqualified.

— You've watched things get smaller when you thought they would grow.

— You've been handed tools that don't make sense for the battle you're facing.

— You've stood surrounded, wondering how anything good could come from this.

But if you've made it this far—trusting God, following His voice, even in tears or confusion—you are proof that His strategy works. Not your strength. Not your plan. His way.

GOD IS NOT JUST STRATEGIC—HE IS SOVEREIGN

He doesn't make decisions by trial and error. His plans are not experiments. They are eternal designs that always lead to glory.

"Many are the plans in the mind of a man, but it is the purpose of the Lord that will stand." —Proverbs 19:21 (ESV)

What God starts, He finishes. What He promises, He performs. What He declares, He fulfills.

"The Lord of hosts has sworn, saying, "Surely, as I have thought, so it shall come to pass, and as I have purposed, so it shall stand:'" —Isaiah 14:24 (NKJV)

You can rest in this: *God is not figuring it out—He already worked it out.*

THE STRATEGY STILL WORKS TODAY

The God of Gideon is still calling men and women out of hiding. He's still breaking jars, raising torches, thinning armies, and confusing the enemy.

He's still fighting battles with worship instead of war cries, with prayers instead of plans, with surrender instead of strength, and He's still using people like you to fulfill His superior strategy on the earth.

DON'T ABANDON THE PROCESS—LEAN INTO IT

You may not always understand God's instructions. But you don't need to.

— You need to trust.
— You need to obey.
— You need to remain in position.
— You need to remember what He promised.

And you need to keep moving, even when His way doesn't make sense, because when the dust settles and the victory is won, you'll look back and realize: *every step made sense from heaven's view.*

REFLECTION QUESTIONS

1. How has your perspective on divine strategy shifted through the life of Gideon?

2. Are there current battles where you need to stop striving and start trusting?

3. How will you apply what you've learned about obedience, brokenness, and spiritual warfare in the days ahead?

DECLARATION

I declare that the superior strategy of God will prevail in my life. I trust His plan above my understanding. I follow His ways, even when they don't make sense. I surrender to His process, knowing He is orchestrating every detail for my good and His glory. I walk by faith, not by sight. Victory belongs to the Lord, and I walk in that victory.

CLOSING PRAYER

Father, thank You for reminding me through Gideon's life that Your strategy never fails. When my eyes can't see it and my heart struggles to believe it, remind me that You are still in control. I surrender my plans, my pride, and my panic. I embrace the unconventional ways You choose to move. Help me never to confuse confusion with chaos, for even in the mystery, You are ordering my steps. Let my life be a testimony that Your strategy is superior. In Jesus' name. Amen.

SCRIPTURE INDEX

GOD'S STRATEGY AND HIS WAYS

- Isaiah 55:8–9
- Proverbs 3:5–6
- Romans 11:33
- 1 Corinthians 1:25

GIDEON'S CALL AND OBEDIENCE

- Judges 6:12–16
- Judges 6:36–40
- Judges 7:1–8
- Judges 7:9–15
- Judges 7:16–22

THE POWER OF WEAKNESS

- 2 Corinthians 12:9–10
- Zechariah 4:6
- 1 Samuel 14:6

FAITH AND TRUST IN GOD

- Hebrews 11:32–34
- Psalm 20:7
- Psalm 37:5
- Hebrews 11:1

GOD USES THE FEW AND THE HUMBLE

- Deuteronomy 7:7–8
- 1 Corinthians 1:27–29
- Micah 6:8

VICTORY BELONGS TO GOD

- Exodus 14:13–14
- 2 Chronicles 20:15
- Romans 8:37
- 1 John 5:4

www.ingramcontent.com/pod-product-compliance
Lightning Source LLC
LaVergne TN
LVHW021542080426
835509LV00019B/2781